It's a Wonderful Life

It's a Wonderful Life

The Fiftieth Anniversary Scrapbook

Jimmy Hawkins

COURAGE
BOOKS

AN IMPRINT OF RUNNING PRESS
PHILADELPHIA • LONDON

9   8   7   6   5   4   3   2
Digit on the right indicates the number of this printing

ISBN 1-56138-767-3

Library of Congress Cataloging-in-Publication Number 96-67166

Picture research by Jimmy Hawkins and Susan Oyama

Photographs provided by Everett Collection: 24, 26–27, 53, 57, 60, 62, 64, 66.
Photographs provided by the Museum of Modern Art/Film Stills Archive: 23, 54, 67, 106.

Published by Courage Books, an imprint of
Running Press Book Publishers
125 South Twenty-second Street
Philadelphia, Pennsylvania 19103-4399

To my mom, Bette, for getting me into the picture business,
and my dad for going along with her.

Acknowledgments

I am indebted to the following institutions and individuals for their assistance and support in the preparation of this book: the Academy of Motion Picture Arts and Sciences; the Donna Reed Foundation, Denison, Iowa; the Frank Capra Archives at Wesleyan University, especially curator Jeanine Basinger and her associate, Leith Johnson; Jay Rubin and the Jimmy Stewart Museum; Brigitte Kueppers and the UCLA Theatre Arts Library; and Ned Comstock and the USC Cinema Television Library. A wonderful salute to Robert Anderson, Grover Asmus, Bud Barnett and Cinema Collectors, Joseph Biroc, Carol Coombs, Ellen Corby, the *Denison Bulletin*, J. Michael Donohew, Eddie Foy III, Paul Gleason, Karolyn Grimes, Albert Hackett, Tommie Hawkins, Todd Karns, Steve Keifer, Elizabeth Kingsley, Bob Lawless, Sheldon Leonard, Virginia Patton Moss, Ned Nalle, Larry Simms, Volta Music, and John Waxman. A special thanks to David Borgenicht, Jeff Day, and most especially Tara Ann McFadden.

It's a Wonderful Life

The Fiftieth Anniversary Scrapbook

Jimmy Hawkins

COURAGE
BOOKS

AN IMPRINT OF RUNNING PRESS
PHILADELPHIA · LONDON

9   8   7   6   5   4   3   2
Digit on the right indicates the number of this printing

ISBN 1-56138-767-3

Library of Congress Cataloging-in-Publication Number 96-67166

Picture research by Jimmy Hawkins and Susan Oyama

Photographs provided by Everett Collection: 24, 26–27, 53, 57, 60, 62, 64, 66.
Photographs provided by the Museum of Modern Art/Film Stills Archive: 23, 54, 67, 106.

Published by Courage Books, an imprint of
Running Press Book Publishers
125 South Twenty-second Street
Philadelphia, Pennsylvania 19103-4399

To my mom, Bette, for getting me into the picture business,
and my dad for going along with her.

Acknowledgments

I am indebted to the following institutions and individuals for their assistance and support in the preparation of this book: the Academy of Motion Picture Arts and Sciences; the Donna Reed Foundation, Denison, Iowa; the Frank Capra Archives at Wesleyan University, especially curator Jeanine Basinger and her associate, Leith Johnson; Jay Rubin and the Jimmy Stewart Museum; Brigitte Kueppers and the UCLA Theatre Arts Library; and Ned Comstock and the USC Cinema Television Library. A wonderful salute to Robert Anderson, Grover Asmus, Bud Barnett and Cinema Collectors, Joseph Biroc, Carol Coombs, Ellen Corby, the *Denison Bulletin*, J. Michael Donohew, Eddie Foy III, Paul Gleason, Karolyn Grimes, Albert Hackett, Tommie Hawkins, Todd Karns, Steve Keifer, Elizabeth Kingsley, Bob Lawless, Sheldon Leonard, Virginia Patton Moss, Ned Nalle, Larry Simms, Volta Music, and John Waxman. A special thanks to David Borgenicht, Jeff Day, and most especially Tara Ann McFadden.

Contents

Preface 8

Introduction 11

The Greatest Gift 13

Frank Capra—The Man Behind the Scenes 14

Jimmy Stewart—George Bailey and Donna Reed—Mary Hatch 40

Lionel Barrymore—Mr. Potter and Henry Travers—Clarence 49

The Bailey Kids 72

Supporting Cast and Crew 78

Life after Life 92

Cast and Crew Credits 94

Preface

I HAD THE PLEASURE OF PLAYING TOMMY BAILEY, THE YOUNGEST OF THE BAILEY CHILDREN, IN *IT'S A WONDERFUL LIFE*. I HAVE FOND MEMORIES OF MAKING THIS CLASSIC PICTURE. I REMEMBER THE SCENE IN WHICH JIMMY STEWART PULLS ME CLOSE TO HIM: I WAS WEARING A SANTA CLAUS MASK, AND EVERY TIME HE HUGGED me the inside of the mask scratched my cheek. And I remember Frank Capra squatting down to explain to me, very patiently, what he wanted me to do. He was a very nice man to this four-year-old kid.

My part took twelve days to shoot. My mom and I would get up very early, around five A.M., and travel by bus and streetcar to the RKO Pathé lot. I had to report to Stage 14 by nine A.M. and would work until five. The lot was in Culver City, just down the street from my favorite studio—MGM. That's where I started my career in the 1943 Spencer Tracy film *The Seventh Cross*. My movie parents were Jessica Tandy and Hume Cronyn—an actual married couple. I also played the son of Lana Turner in *Marriage Is a Private Affair*. I worked in other movies with such greats as Katharine Hepburn, Greer Garson, Robert Young, and even Lassie.

After *It's a Wonderful Life,* when television was still new, I was cast in the ABC family show *The Ruggles,* starring Charlie Ruggles. In 1953 Gene Autry cast me as Tagg Oakley in the Annie Oakley series, a role I played until 1958. About that time Donna Reed was looking for someone to play the boyfriend of her television daughter, Shelley Fabares. I was signed and was still doing the series when it ended eight years later. In 1969 I became a producer, making the film *Evel Knievel* with George Hamilton and Sue Lyon.

Through the years I maintained a relationship with Donna Reed. If she heard I was producing a movie, she would drop me a line or we'd meet for lunch. I visited her in the hospital and at home until a week before she died. I'll always remember her soft touch from *It's a Wonderful Life* and the same feeling of her hand touching my cheek as I leaned down to kiss her goodbye for the last time on Christmas Day 1985.

In 1986 I became involved with the Donna Reed Foundation for the Performing Arts. The foundation awards scholarships to talented individuals who wish to pursue a career in the arts. Shelley Fabares invited me to be a part of shaping what has become an annual nine-day festival in Donna's hometown, Denison, Iowa. It's not hard to understand how Donna Reed made the character of Mary Bailey ring so true—it's because of the values the citizens of this great town instilled in her.

"Each man's life touches so many other lives. If he wasn't around, it would leave an awful hole." —Clarence

The Frank Capra Archives has received hundreds of letters from people who were suicidal before watching *It's a Wonderful Life* and have been touched by its message.

I've kept in touch with many members of the cast of *It's a Wonderful Life* and have had opportunities to interview them. Many have shared stories of people telling them how the movie touched their lives; I've heard similar stories from the Donna Reed Foundation and the Jimmy Stewart Museum. It just goes to show how important movies are. As Frank Capra once said, "You get a chance to speak to millions of people in the dark."

This book is my tribute to Frank Capra and to the cast and crew of *It's a Wonderful Life*.

Jimmy Stewart with Jimmy Hawkins at cast picnic.

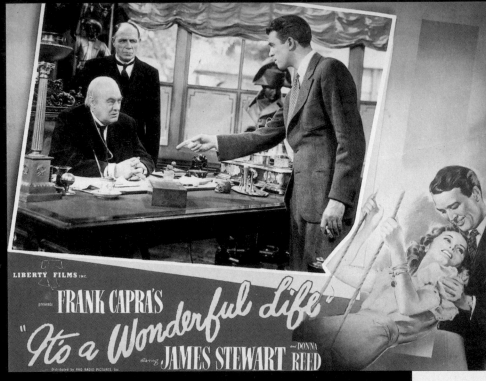

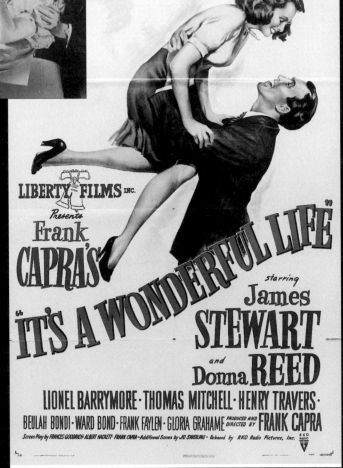

Introduction

What would life be like without George Bailey running down the streets of Bedford Falls and yelling "Merry Christmas!"? What would life be like without the Bailey family and the residents of Bedford Falls singing "Auld Lang Syne" around the Christmas tree? What would life be like without Zuzu's petals?

"It's a Wonderful Life" has become as much a holiday classic as Christmas shopping and baking cookies. Soon after opening in December 1946, the film captured five Academy Award nominations: Best Picture, Best Director, Best Actor, Best Film Editing, and Best Sound. It didn't win any Oscars but it captured the hearts of millions of Americans.

Now, fifty years later, not a day goes by that the Frank Capra Archives, the Donna Reed Foundation, and the Library of Congress don't receive an inquiry about "It's a Wonderful Life." It has become the American version of "A Christmas Carol," our message of personal struggle and hope. In the following pages, you'll meet the people responsible for making "It's a Wonderful Life" everyone's favorite holiday classic.

The Greatest Gift

THE MOST BELOVED MOVIE OF OUR TIME DESCRIBES THE LIFE OF A COMMON MAN, A SMALL-TOWN MAN WHO WORKED AND LIVED SO HE COULD MARRY HIS SWEETHEART AND GIVE HIS FAMILY "A COUPLE OF DECENT ROOMS AND A BATH." IT'S FITTING THAT THE INSPIRATION FOR THIS MAN'S STORY OCCURRED during a simple, everyday task. On February 12, 1938, Philip Van Doren Stern was shaving when an idea about a man who contemplates suicide came to him. This discouraged, ordinary man wishes he had never been born. When his guardian angel is sent down from heaven to help him, he is given a special gift—the gift of seeing how different his family, friends, and the people in his community would have been without him. Van Doren Stern finished shaving, wrote a two-page treatment, and set it aside for five years.

Van Doren Stern, an accomplished writer and historian, would occasionally share the idea with friends, and they encouraged him to write more. When he added the Christmas theme and titled it "The Greatest Gift," it just seemed right to him. He sent his story to various magazines but received only rejections. Still fond of "The Greatest Gift," he revised it, had it made into a pamphlet, and sent it to two hundred friends as a Christmas card.

One friend, Hollywood agent Shirley Collier, called after receiving the card and told him the story had the makings of a movie. Van Doren Stern agreed to let Collier try to drum up the interest of a producer or a studio, but he confessed to his wife that he thought the agent was crazy.

In 1943, RKO Pictures bought the rights to "The Greatest Gift" for $10,000. The story appeared in *Good Housekeeping* later that year under the title "The Man Who Never Was" and was also published as a small book titled *The Greatest Gift*. After RKO purchased the rights, though, Van Doren Stern's involvement ended. He was disappointed that Capra always referred to his story as "this little Christmas card," and felt he should have received more credit from Capra.

Frank Capra—The Man Behind the Scenes

FRANK CAPRA CAPTURED THE AMERICAN VOICE IN HIS MORE THAN SIXTY FILMS AS A PRODUCER, DIRECTOR, AND SCREENWRITER. HE IS REMEMBERED AS A PERFECTIONIST WITH A GENIUS FOR THE SPOKEN WORD.

IN 1945, AFTER YEARS OF BEING UNDER EXCLUSIVE CONTRACT TO HARRY COHN at Columbia Pictures and serving in World War II, he formed Liberty Films with three partners—William Wyler, George Stevens, and Sam Briskin. As independent filmmakers, they pledged to make films that rose above typical Hollywood fare. Liberty Films, whose offices were located on the RKO lot, was founded on three major principles:

A strong story, not just a film with stars.

Quality from an artistic and entertainment standpoint.

Costs will not be exploited as an indication of the entertainment value of a film.

Capra was grappling with a number of early Liberty projects when Charles Koerner, the head of RKO, told him about "The Greatest Gift." Capra read it and thought it was the greatest idea he had ever heard. On September 1, 1945, RKO sold "The Greatest Gift" and three screen adaptations it had commissioned to Liberty Films for $50,000. Capra read all three versions, but none captured what he had read in the Christmas card.

Capra immediately hired Francis Goodrich and Albert Hackett to write a new adaptation. Over the course of filming Capra brought in several other writers to polish the script. Writers Guild files show that screen credit was given to Francis Goodrich, Albert Hackett, and Frank Capra, with additional scenes by Jo Swerling. Michael Wilson, who polished the script, was credited as a "contributor to screenplay"; Dorothy Parker, who also did a polish, was given no credit.

Next, Capra began casting his movie. Cary Grant, who had convinced RKO to buy the rights to the story, was the studio's first choice to play George Bailey. Capra had his own vision and when he stepped in he wiped the slate clean: Jimmy Stewart was his first and only choice. Capra, who had first worked with

14

Wonderful Reviews

**THE HOLLYWOOD REPORTER,
DECEMBER 11, 1946**

The Capra show is fine and clean, heart-wringing in spots, and in others, hilariously funny. . . . It's the greatest of all Capra pictures, and in saying that, one must mean one of the greatest pictures of this or any other year.

UNITED PRESS

Never in all my years of covering Hollywood have I been so moved by a movie as by It's a Wonderful Life. *The Capra film is the season's climax.*

**BOX OFFICE DIGEST,
DECEMBER 19, 1946**

Frank Capra is back with a bang. It's a Wonderful Life *is an all-American picture—that goes for caliber and its appeal—a picture that is both an enjoyable and an enriching entertainment experience.*

**NEW YORK SUN,
DECEMBER 21, 1946**

Last night the Globe Theatre presented Broadway moviegoers with their finest Christmas present, a warm and merry comedy called It's a Wonderful Life.

**LOS ANGELES HERALD EXPRESS,
DECEMBER 26, 1946**

Frank Capra's It's a Wonderful Life *melted all the barnacles off my heart and left me feeling young and full of ideals again.*

**NEW YORK DAILY NEWS,
JANUARY 18, 1947**

We've seldom seen such a moving and inspiring entertaining and exciting picture as this one.

**CHICAGO HERALD AMERICAN,
DECEMBER 27, 1946**

A glorious picture for the holiday season. . . . This one has the substance of which great movies are made.

**TIME,
JANUARY 20, 1947**

Producer-Director Frank Capra and Actor James Stewart stage a triumphant Hollywood homecoming.

**LIFE,
DECEMBER 30, 1946**

Movie of the Week . . . a masterful edifice of comedy and sentiment.

**NEWSWEEK,
DECEMBER 30, 1946**

A film in the old Capra manner.

**HOUSTON POST,
MARCH 7, 1947**

A movie of superlative value . . . bringing a human drama of essential truth.

Stewart on *You Can't Take It With You,* recognized that the actor's warmth, humor, and underlying strength were perfect for George Bailey, the character who'd come to personify the American common man.

Capra liked Jean Arthur for the part of George's wife, Mary Bailey, but she wasn't available. (She later said she was glad she hadn't done the film—her loss.) The director's second choice was Ginger Rogers, who thought the part too bland; other actresses Capra considered privately included Olivia De Havilland, Martha Scott, and Ann Dvorak. Finally Capra decided on Donna Reed, whose sensible, farm-girl appeal impressed him; he thought she looked like a one-man woman.

There was one snag: Reed, like most actors of the era, was under contract to another studio—MGM. Capra had to bargain with MGM to use her in the film. With Reed signed, Capra now had the key players for the Bailey family—a couple that would dance together, sing love songs, raise a family, and be hard-working citizens.

Assembling the rest of the cast, many of whom had worked with Capra before, was a relatively easy task. MGM loaned Lionel Barrymore for the part of Mr. Potter, and Henry Travers was the only actor considered for the role of Clarence Oddbody, Angel Second Class.

Thomas Mitchell, who played the part of absent-minded Uncle Billy, had first worked with Capra on *Lost Horizon* in 1937. In 1939 Mitchell had received a Best Supporting Actor Award for *Stagecoach* and appeared as Scarlett's father, Gerald O'Hara, in *Gone With the Wind.* The final film for both Mitchell and Capra was *Pocketful of Miracles* in 1961.

The genius of Frank Capra was evident in the casting of H. B. Warner as Old Mr. Gower. Warner had been the victim of typecasting since portraying Jesus Christ in Cecil B. DeMille's *King of Kings.* Capra was not worried about typecasting and was rewarded with a stunning performance from Warner. Warner described Gower as "the damnedest dirtiest bum you ever saw. In all my films before I have always been offered mostly roles with great dignity." Warner's risk paid off. The remainder of the cast were Capra's stock players.

Filming began on April 15, 1946, at Beverly Hills High School. (The school boasted an actual pool under the gymnasium floor.) The film was budgeted at $2,362,427 for eighty-four days of shooting; it ended up four days over schedule and way over budget, at a final tally of $3,180,000.

It's a Wonderful Life was due to be released on January 30, 1947. However, RKO's *Sinbad the Sailor* didn't have enough Technicolor prints ready for its Christmas release, so *It's a*

Wonderful Life was rushed to the theaters. It premiered on December 20, 1946, at New York's Globe Theatre. A ticket cost $1.25, plus tax.

When Oscar time came along, Frank Capra's *It's a Wonderful Life* received five nominations but won none. Capra, however, won a Golden Globe award for Best Director. The winner for Best Picture was *The Best Years of Our Lives,* directed by Capra's Liberty Films partner William Wyler.

The movie lost $480,000 and was ranked 27th on Variety's list of 1946–1947 releases. On May 16, 1947, Liberty Films was sold to Paramount Pictures.

AN INTERVIEW WITH FRANK CAPRA

Not only did I have the honor of working on a film with Frank Capra, but I also had spent time with him one on one on several occasions. On November 2, 1968, we met at the Academy of Motion Picture Arts and Sciences for a screening of *It's a Wonderful Life.*

Jimmy Hawkins: How did you choose us kids for *It's a Wonderful Life*?

Frank Capra: I had interviews. I think every kid in Hollywood was there. Then I started matching—"This kid looks good with that kid." Then we got you all together to see how you looked with Jimmy Stewart and Donna Reed. Then I felt I had the Bailey family. I didn't read any of you. Just instincts, a hunch! And, may I add, you were great in it.

Hawkins: Thank you. I remember saying that "excuse me" line, and how you crouched down to explain what you wanted from me. I was only four years old at the time. But I remember you said, "Say 'excuse me' here, here, and here." I actually knew at four that I didn't do exactly what you asked, that I missed saying "excuse me" once and there was a lull in the scene. Why didn't you shoot it over?

Capra: I think we had filmed that scene two or three times. I find the more an actor does it, the less tense he is. He becomes more human. That take felt real, so I printed it. You know, the "excuse me" line wasn't in the script. I added it the night before. I felt it would help break the tension that was going on in the scene.

Hawkins: What was the most difficult scene to shoot?

Capra: The scene with you kids, when Stewart comes in and raises hell. I had all this drama going on, and I'm playing it with laughs! If you play it too funny, the audience will think they have to laugh at the drama. That gave me the most trouble.

Hawkins: Is *It's a Wonderful Life* really your favorite film?

Capra: Yes, it is . . . .

Above: Director Frank Capra and Jimmy Stewart on the set of "It's a Wonderful Life."

A Pictorial Retelling of "It's a Wonderful Life" . . .

A young Mary Hatch (Jean Gale) looks on as Violet (Jeanine Ann Roose) attempts to charm George (Bobbie Anderson).

Old Man Gower (H. B. Warner) after learning his son has died.

Left: Mr. Gower sends George off on an errand.

Above: Uncle Billy (Thomas Mitchell) tells George not to disturb his father.

Even a young George Bailey is not afraid to stand up to the villainous Mr. Potter (Lionel Barrymore).

Left: George and Mr. Gower say goodbye before George plans to see the world.

Above: As the Bailey men discuss life and the Building & Loan, George expresses his admiration for his father.

Actor, Carl Switzer, best known for his role of Alfalfa in "The Little Rascals," cannot compete with George Bailey for Mary's affection.

Left: George and Mary (Donna Reed) dance
the Charleston before getting soaked.
Above: George and Mary sing "Buffalo Gals."

Left: George tells Mary his wishes and dreams.

Above: Mary hides in the hydrangeas while George considers being a gentleman.

George's conviction saves the Building & Loan.

Jimmy Stewart—George Bailey and Donna Reed—Mary Hatch

THROUGHOUT HIS CAREER, JIMMY STEWART STARRED IN MORE THAN SEVENTY-FIVE FILMS AND RECEIVED A BEST ACTOR ACADEMY AWARD, FOR HIS ROLE AS A HARD-BITTEN REPORTER IN *THE PHILADELPHIA STORY*. STEWART WAS ALSO A WAR HERO WHO WAS HONORED WITH THE CROIX DE GUERRE AND SEVEN BATTLE STARS.

Over the years I've spoken with Jimmy Stewart at the Warner Bros. studio, Hollywood functions, Donna Reed's funeral, and the Frank Capra memorial, among other occasions. We'd often discuss his stories relating to *It's a Wonderful Life*. Here are my memories of those special conversations:

Jimmy Hawkins: How did you get involved in *Life*?

Jimmy Stewart: Well, it had been almost five years since I had done a movie in Hollywood. The war changed things. I'd been home for a few months with no offers, just killed time with Hank Fonda. We'd hang around and fly kites—stuff like that. I got so insecure that I actually thought of going back home to Indiana, Pennsylvania, to run my dad's store. One day Frank Capra called and said he had an idea that he wanted to talk to me about. I went to see him. I remember Sam Briskin [Capra's partner] and Lew Wasserman [Stewart's agent] were there.

Frank started the story—something about me committing suicide, a guardian angel, and my character wishing he'd never been born. He talked and talked. It was pretty confusing.

Finally, Capra stopped talking. He said, "It doesn't sound very good, does it?" I told him if he wanted me to do this story about an angel with no wings and me wishing I was never born, "I'm your boy!"

Hawkins: That's how you decided to do the film?

Stewart: Well, I had done a couple of my best pictures with Frank. I knew if Frank wanted me to do *It's a Wonderful Life,* I was in good hands. I had complete confidence in him. I liked the story because it was about an average guy. And there weren't enough stories about average guys.

Hawkins: Some actors think average guys are dull.

Stewart: They don't have to be. A character who takes dope

and beats his wife can be dull too. I always wanted to be in movies that are worthwhile for people to see.

Hawkins: Well, *It's a Wonderful Life* is certainly worthwhile.

Stewart: That was Frank Capra's hope, and my hope too. It's the kind of picture I wanted to make more of.

Hawkins: What was it like when you started shooting?

Stewart: It was a great cast—Henry Travers, Thomas Mitchell, Beulah Bondi [she had played Stewart's mom before], and Donna Reed, who was very special. And Ward Bond, Frank Faylen, Samuel Hinds, Mary Treen—real solid performers. And of course Lionel Barrymore! He really helped me with my doubts. I wasn't sure if doing movies and acting were important enough, coming out of the war and all. Maybe Barrymore sensed something. He really helped lift my spirits. He reminded me that acting is important. Millions of people see you, and it helps shape their lives. Your acting has that kind of influence.

I asked him if acting was decent. Barrymore brought me to reality when he said, "Is it more decent to drop a bomb on people or bring a ray of sunshine to them through your acting?" He was right! I had a great gift. Things were better after that. I felt I belonged.

Hawkins: What do you remember most about *Life*?

Stewart: I remember how well prepared Frank Capra was. He knew what he wanted. He'd always let us try the scene our way. Then he would build on it. He'd offer suggestions and say "Try it this way" or "Do it like this."

Hawkins: Was it your favorite movie?

Stewart: Yep! And most of the mail I get is about *It's a Wonderful Life.*

Hawkins: I remember the *It's a Wonderful Life* picnic. I won the watermelon-eating contest. I have a picture that was taken of everyone at the picnic, and you're at both ends of the picture. Do you remember how that happened?

Stewart: Sure. The picnic was kind of our wrap party. Frank and I put it on out near Lake Malibu. We wanted everyone to have a photo of it.

We all gathered around—over three hundred, I think! Back then still cameras didn't have wide-angle lenses, so the camera would have to pan the whole group. Well, Frank and I were at one end, then when the camera panned across the group the cameraman yelled, "Go!" Frank and I ducked down and ran behind everyone and ended up on the other side. When the photo was developed, it looked like we were standing at both ends of the picture. That was Frank's idea. He always added something extra to a picture.

Hawkins: What do you think of colorizing *Life*?

"Indiana, Pennsylvania: It's a Wonderful Life"

By Jay Rubin, President of the board of directors of the Jimmy Stewart Museum

Nestled in the hills of western Pennsylvania is a community that begs comparison with Bedford Falls. It is a community of 16,000 people. Indiana, Pennsylvania, is more than your typical American small town; it embodies all the values that small-town America represents. Patriotism isn't just a word, it's a way of life. Church socials are events. Service clubs abound, and neighborhood picnics are part of the summer ritual. Boys and girls are active in scouting, local politicians still kiss babies, and everyone knows everyone else. Indiana is a town filled with George and Mary Baileys, Uncle Billys, and cops like Bert.

Indiana is not unlike many other rural communities, except that it boasts the birthplace of the one and only true George Bailey: Jimmy Stewart. James Maitland Stewart was born on May 20, 1908, and his father ran the local hardware store, where Jimmy spent many hours during his youth.

Although Jimmy Stewart went off to Hollywood to become one of its greatest actors, he has never been forgotten in his hometown. The values instilled in him by his parents and the community were the same values portrayed in "It's a Wonderful Life" and the people of Bedford Falls. The admiration that Jimmy has for his hometown is returned a thousand times over by its citizens, who are proud of their favorite son. In 1983, on the occasion of Stewart's 75th birthday, the community gathered together, as the world looked on, to erect a statue in honor of him. Stewart proudly appeared to acknowledge their affection.

While the statue is a fitting tribute to Jimmy Stewart, the residents of Indiana felt that Stewart's life and career deserved more than more that. They wanted to present a living tribute to the man who exemplified the values of the community.

On May 20, 1995, the Jimmy Stewart Museum was dedicated. Stewart's two daughters, Kelly Harcourt and Judy Merrill, were on hand for the tribute. The museum is of modest proportions—as requested by the honoree—and is situated on the third floor of the Indiana County Free Library building on the corner of Ninth and Philadelphia Streets. The site of the museum is appropriate and particularly pleasing to Mr. Stewart. You can look out different windows of the museum and observe his boyhood home, his statue in front of the courthouse, the former location of the hardware store, and the famous clock pictured on the 1945 cover of "Life" magazine with Jimmy in the foreground. The museum is composed of six galleries, a theater, and a gift shop. There are hundreds of photos and posters, memorabilia, and other articles representative of Jimmy Stewart's career in both the entertainment field and the military. Stewart has graciously provided items from his own collection. Original scripts, costumes, awards, photographs, and other unique mementos of his glorious career can be found here. The theater has fifty seats and a state-of-the-art audio visual system, donated by friends at Universal City Studios. The museum takes pride in displaying "It's a Wonderful Life" memorabilia. A visitor can find posters, photographs, advertisements, and cast autographs on display.

In 1995 the museum celebrated its first Christmas with a celebration held in honor of "It's a Wonderful Life." The community of Indiana, also holds an "It's a Wonderful Life, Christmas" celebration. To understand the meaning of the event it is important to note that Indiana county is known as the Christmas tree capital of the world. In 1993, several members of the cast and crew visited Indiana to help celebrate "It's a Wonderful Life, Christmas," and they left the community understanding that Jimmy Stewart was not so much George Bailey, but George Bailey represented the goodness of Jimmy Stewart.

Stewart: I don't like it! The movie loses something. It's flat. But the new generation doesn't like black-and-white. So I guess if that's what it takes to get young people to watch it and get that wonderful message, so be it. But it's not for me!

At the Frank Capra Memorial, Jimmy Stewart made a moving tribute. He summed it all up in his final farewell: "Frank Capra has a special place in my heart. He is responsible for my career as an actor. Thank you, Frank."

THE JIMMY STEWART MUSEUM

Indiana, Pennsylvania's favorite son sent a recorded message to his hometown for a reunion in 1993. His voice cracked with age and emotion when he spoke in an eerie philosophical way that seemed to sum up not only what he thought of *It's a Wonderful Life*, but his philosophy of life itself.

The enduring message of hope, charity, and life renewed is so important in trying times—when money is tight and holding the family together can be difficult. As George Bailey learned, what really counts in life are the things you can't put a price tag on: family, friends, and the belief in miracles. Stewart wished the people of Indiana, Pennsylvania, love and happiness and all the joys and wonders of a wonderful life.

DONNA REED

Star of the long-running series *The Donna Reed Show,* Donna Reed exemplified the quality of wholesomeness. It is ironic that her greatest screen triumph, her Academy Award for Best Supporting Actress, was gained by playing a prostitute in *From Here to Eternity* in 1953.

Jimmy Hawkins: What do you remember most about *It's a Wonderful Life*?

Donna Reed: I remember we used to call you Rip Van Winkle. You could sleep anywhere, anytime. When we were ready to shoot they would wake you up and you were ready to go. It was really quite cute.

Hawkins: How did you get the part of Mary?

Reed: The way I heard it, Frank Capra saw me in the John Ford film *They Were Expendable,* with John Wayne. He liked the way I played the Navy nurse. I was under contract to MGM, and they loaned me out to Capra's company.

Hawkins: What was it like on the set of *Life*?

Reed: It was the hardest I've ever worked—but it was fun! Capra had me do things I had never done before. I was singing, dancing, and doing comedy. I went from a teenager to a woman of forty. I was twenty-five when I did *It's a Wonderful Life*.

Hawkins: How were Stewart and Capra to work with?

Reed: They were always kind. This was their first movie after the war. They wondered if they still had it—I think they were nervous. Capra was always quick to laugh. He was always making things up, adding funny bits that weren't in the script.

Hawkins: Did any of your Iowa upbringing help you out?

Reed: Well, it made me fifty extra dollars. Lionel Barrymore bet me fifty dollars that I couldn't milk a cow. When I was a little girl growing up on our farm, we kids had to milk the cows every morning before we left for school. Mr. Capra asked one of the wranglers to bring a cow over, and I milked it right there and then. Everyone got a big laugh out of it, even Mr. Barrymore. That was the easiest money I ever made.

Hawkins: What are some other memories you have of working on the film?

Reed: I remember standing in the living room for the final scene and thinking as the camera panned the entire group. The room was filled with all these wonderful character actors singing "Auld Lang Syne." I felt very special to belong to that group.

Hawkins: If you had a chance to do it over, would you do anything differently as Mary?

Reed: No. I played it the way Frank Capra wanted it. However, he told me that in the part when George had never been born he should have made Mary more independent and attractive instead of playing her as the frightened, weak librarian.

Hawkins: Was Frank Capra nice to work with?

Reed: Not only nice, but very kind and giving. I remember during the filming I asked for permission to fly to Chicago to adopt a little girl. He worked the schedule around so I could. He was a very sweet man.

I remember that Donna Reed was also very giving. We would talk on the phone, write letters, and have lunch over the years. I remember having dinner with her in 1984 at Shelley Fabares's engagement party. She looked wonderful. Who could have guessed that she would be gone in a year.

Donna Reed touched the lives of so many. The Donna Reed Foundation, set up by her friends and family, continues this legacy even today. The Foundation is headquartered in Donna's hometown, Denison, Iowa. Every year there is a nine-day festival with workshops for the performing arts. Professional actors and actresses come from Hollywood and New York to instruct the students. The festival ends with the awarding of a $10,000 scholarship to an individual with a desire to pursue an education and career in the performing arts.

The cast and crew assemble for a group shot at the "It's a Wonderful Life" picnic hosted by Capra and Stewart.

Left:
Henry Travers,
as Clarence.

Right:
Lionel Barrymore,
as Mr. Potter.

Lionel Barrymore—Mr. Potter and Henry Travers—Clarence

LIONEL BARRYMORE WAS A VERY NICE AND GENTLE MAN. DURING THE MOVIE BREAKS, I WOULD SIT ON HIS LAP AND RIDE AROUND IN HIS WHEELCHAIR. I HAD THE PLEASURE OF WORKING WITH HIM TWICE AFTER *IT'S A WONDERFUL LIFE*, IN *DUEL IN THE SUN* (1946) AND *DOWN TO THE SEA IN SHIPS* (1949).

Lionel Barrymore began his career in films in 1909. His versatility enabled him to play everything from romantic leads to villains. It was in the 1920s when he began to play the parts of older men, a type of character he would continue to perfect over the rest of his acting career. His severe arthritis made acting possible only if he were on crutches or sitting down.

In 1926 he signed with MGM. This twenty-nine-year alliance was the longest actor-studio association in MGM's history. It started with *The Barrier* and ended in 1953 with *Main Street to Broadway*. MGM kept Barrymore on salary until his death in 1954. He appeared in more than 250 films and won a Best Actor Oscar in 1930 for *A Free Soul*. Widely known for his roles as Dr. Gillespie in the Dr. Kildaire series, Barrymore also made a highly successful directorial debut at MGM in 1929 with *Malcolm X*.

Frank Capra said, "Lionel Barrymore is in any actor's Hall of Fame." His name deserved top billing among the immortals, but he was the humblest, most cooperative actor that Capra knew. They first worked together in 1938 on Columbia's *You Can't Take It With You* (also starring Jimmy Stewart), which earned Capra Oscars for Best Picture and Best Director.

HENRY TRAVERS

"It was fascinating. It was just a joy to see him work and to work with him," Jimmy Stewart said of Travers.

Travers originally worked the British stage and made the move to Broadway in the 1920s. He started his film career with *Reunion in Vienna* in 1933. Capra also considered Travers for other roles in *It's a Wonderful Life*—Peter Bailey, George's father; Uncle Billy; and Old Man Gower. But Henry Travers's voice and kind-looking face helped bring Clarence a magical and heavenly quality that Capra felt was unique.

In an interview, Jimmy Stewart praised Travers's wit: "There couldn't have been anybody better than Henry Travers as Clarence, there just couldn't. His timing, his looks, and the way he played it straight. You could see him absolutely guarding himself against anything that would be a comic-strip type of thing. Because he was an angel. He didn't have any wings, but he was an angel."

Travers made more than fifty films during his lifetime. His last film, in 1949, was *Girl from Jones Beach*. He received an Academy Award nomination for his role of Mr. Ballard in *Mrs. Miniver*. Diehard Travers fans will realize that *The Bells of St. Mary's,* which appears on the Bedford Falls movie marquee, also starred Henry Travers.

How Movies Touch Our Lives

The theme to "It's a Wonderful Life" can be found in the lives of many.

Robert McFarlane, the former U.S. National Security Advisor was very candid in telling how "It's a Wonderful Life" helped him overcome depression that led to an attempted suicide. He told the "New York Times" that after he saw the film he could identify with George Bailey and understand the importance of each person and their role in humanity.

Another example is illustrated by a man in Florida who was charged with the attempted murder of his critically ill wife. He then planned to turn the gun on himself and take his own life. The man told a judge that the "world would be a better place without me." The judge was moved by the man's feeling of worthlessness and ordered him to watch "It's a Wonderful Life." As a result the charges were dropped.

While awaiting Harry's return, George tells Uncle Billy about his plans to see the world.

On George's "unplanned" walk, his thoughts are pleasantly interrupted.

A stunning Mary watches George from her second-story window.

Above: Mrs. Hatch (Sarah Edwards) casts a skeptical eye on George.

Right: George and Mary's romance takes off.

The newlyweds are sent off on their honeymoon.

Left: George and Mary witness the run on the bank.

Above: The honeymoon is put on hold as Ernie (Frank Faylen), George, and Mary see the panic.

Left: Mr. Potter takes control of the bank but the Building & Loan is out of his reach.

George's glowing bride in the house of her dreams.

The newlyweds embrace.

Above: The Baileys move the Martini family to Bailey Park.

Right: "Hee-Haw!" It's Sam Wainwright (Frank Albertson) and his bride (Marian Carr) returning to their humble roots.

George is astounded when Mr. Potter offers him the salary and job of a lifetime.

Mr. Potter is once more amazed at George's loyalty to the people of Bedford Falls.

The Bailey Kids

KAROLYN GRIMES—ZUZU BAILEY

Jimmy Hawkins: What's the first thing you remember about *It's a Wonderful Life*?

Karolyn Grimes: Going to the studio for the interview. My mom got a call from my agent, Lola Moore, and we drove out to Culver City after school to meet the casting agent. We'd always go after school unless it was a weekend. My mom didn't want me to miss my classes.

Hawkins: Is that when you met Mr. Capra?

Grimes: I don't remember. There were three or four gentlemen in the room, so he was probably one of them. But I do remember that at the interview the mother of one of the other girls spilled coffee on my dress. My mother told me when I was older that that mother used to do things like that to make the other girl cry and feel funny when she went in to meet the casting director. But I just used it as something to talk about. I guess the casting director thought it was really natural, because out of all those kids they chose me to be Zuzu.

Hawkins: What comes to mind about being on the set of *Life*?

Grimes: Your mom. She was always knitting. She would always have a box of animal crackers for you—something to keep you busy, I guess. You and I didn't have to go to school, so we would play together a lot. I would chase you around the stage. We'd sneak around the set and look at the decorated Christmas tree. It was huge! My mom caught us once and warned us not to touch it. After we finished filming the prop man gave me a couple of ornaments as souvenirs, but over the years they were lost.

Hawkins: Tell the story about your room in the movie.

Grimes: It was very confusing to a six-year-old. Zuzu's room was supposed to be upstairs. We'd run upstairs and go into the room, but when we went through the door there was no room, just a landing. The room we shot in was actually on the ground level in the corner of the same sound stage.

Hawkins: What do you think of the movie's popularity?

Grimes: It's really been a bright spot in my life. You know, my mom and dad died when I was young, and I was raised by an uncle in Missouri. I had lost all contact with friends and neighbors. But because of the popularity of the movie I wrote an article for a local newspaper. The Associated Press picked it up and it ran all over the United States. One day I got a call from a man who had read the story, and he turned out to be my dad's

The Bailey family (clockwise from top): Jimmy Stewart, Donna Reed, Carol Coombs, Jimmy Hawkins, Karolyn Grimes, and Larry Simms.

best friend. Somebody else read it and told the story to a friend in California who turned out to be my next-door neighbor. They both told me stories and all sorts of things that I never knew about my family. If it wasn't for *It's a Wonderful Life* those people would never have found me.

I don't know why I was chosen for that part. Maybe I was chosen for perhaps a lifetime career of touching other lives. People who love the movie have taken me into their hearts and made me feel so fortunate to be surrounded by so much love. I made many movies as a child, but there are only a couple I remember well.

Hawkins: How has being a part of *It's a Wonderful Life* enriched your life?

Grimes: The movie is about friendship and touching lives. I have been able to enrich my world with friends everywhere I go. I feel so lucky to have people care. My husband of twenty-five years died in 1994. That Christmas I received seventy-five cards from a wonderful group in Pennsylvania. That was just one kind gesture that happens constantly. Each year I go more places as Zuzu, and I meet many young people who are trying to make a difference. This movie has given them the tool to work with.

Hawkins: Have you started a hobby or collection as a result of *It's a Wonderful Life*?

Grimes: Oh, yes. Fans have started giving me angels, because "every time a bell rings an angel gets its wings." So I've started collecting them. Now I look at these precious miniatures and feel very special having been a part of *It's a Wonderful Life*.

CAROL COOMBS—JANIE BAILEY

Jimmy Hawkins: How did you get started in the motion-picture business?

Carol Coombs: I'm originally from Canada. My mother brought us to Los Angeles when I was four. I remember her getting my brother and me an agent, Lola Moore, and then we started to go on interviews.

Hawkins: How did you like the interviews?

Coombs: They were scary and intimidating. Sometimes I would leave feeling rejected and sad. Of course, if I got the part it was terrific. I loved going to makeup and hairdressing and wardrobe. I felt like I was being glamorized.

Hawkins: What do you remember about going to the studio?

Coombs: Eating at the studio commissary, being surrounded by stars and important people. It was enjoyable and thrilling! I loved getting out of "real school classes" and doing assignments on the studio lot with other kids in films.

Hawkins: How did they make you cry for the movie?

The "It's a Wonderful Life" Sequel

By Ned Nalle, executive Vice President, Universal Television

An embarrassing thing happened in 1985 when I was late meeting Frank Capra for dinner. He was visiting from La Quinta to discuss his story for the sequel to "It's a Wonderful Life."

I ran up to the maitre'd at the restaurant of a venerable hotel in Beverly Hills and asked to be directed to Mr. Capra's table. I was informed that policy dictated that incomplete parties were not to be seated. Accordingly, my host was relegated to sit alone in a holding area near the bar. Embarrassed and outraged, I strongly informed the maitre'd that Frank Capra should not be made to wait for a table under any circumstance. Icily, the lady behind the desk wondered aloud "Who is Frank Capra?" I sputtered out a filmography, but the legacy non-plussed her . . . until I got to "It's a Wonderful Life."

"Oh," was her embarrassed reply. "Someone should have told me." We were quickly shown to a table.

Frank Capra and I had become pen pals ten years before when he was touring college campuses promoting "The Name Above the Title." I interviewed him at the time for my radio show on Princeton's undergraduate-run station.

About the same time, the movie and television studio I would later work for (Universal) had acquired remake and sequel rights to "It's a Wonderful Life" to produce the Marlo Thomas television movie "It Happened One Christmas." As Mr. Capra was not involved with that production he did request that he be awarded creative control over any other "It's a Wonderful Life" sequels. However, he did stipulate that we could not require him to direct, as one of his eyes "wasn't working as well as it did in '46."

He handed me his outline, "Citizen or Slave: A Chronology of Scenes for the Sequel to It's A Wonderful Life." Penned by Capra, the treatment opens with Uncle Billy's crow leading the audience to a dejected George Bailey apologizing to his father's portrait about another imminent demise of the Bailey Brothers Building & Loan.

Many of the original characters return. Zuzu is now in law school but her brother Tom, ran away from home at twelve.

Alarmingly, Bedford Falls has been plagued with a terrorist attack on both its biggest factory and the Bailey's church.

In an ironic moment in the treatment, Mr. Potter finds religion before passing away at the age of ninety-eight. Nevertheless, he is buried with both fists clutching $100 bills, attempting to become as Mr. Capra told me with a wink, "the first person to prove you can take it with you!"

At Christmas, a long-lost Tom comes home and surprises the family with a visit bringing a miraculous solution to the Building & Loan woes, a one million dollar government bailout. The catch is that the government is seizing the Bailey property by eminent domain, and Tom is now a lawyer working for them. But George realizes he is being forced to sell and that no government windfalls are available for his neighbors and customers.

An equally incensed Zuzu rushes home from law school to help George argue against her estranged brother and the U.S. Government. Despite reversal, George and Zuzu defend the rights of the citizens of Bedford Falls all the way to the Supreme Court.

Without giving away the entire ending, suffice it to say that Zuzu's juris doctorate is ultimately earned outside of the classroom.

Unfortunately, this sequel has never been produced, as we were not successful in convincing a cable network to commission it at the time. When Mr. Capra fell ill the project went dormant. Probably forever.

Coombs: They prepared us, told us what our emotions should be, but I really didn't have to act. Jimmy Stewart scared me, breaking up the house and everything—he was fantastic!

Hawkins: When you met Frank Capra did you have to play the piano for him?

Coombs: No, thank goodness. But I did have the ability to play somewhat. Obviously if I had had to play well, they would have had to hire somebody else. I'm so grateful they didn't!

I was very frightened. It was stressful! I had to practice really hard. I didn't want to make any mistakes. I didn't want the cameraman to say stop because I made a mistake. I tried really hard. It was such an honor to be associated with the film.

LARRY SIMMS—PETE BAILEY

Hawkins: What do you remember about *It's a Wonderful Life*?

Larry Simms: I remember talking to the sound technicians. Every chance I got I would spend my spare time asking them questions and learning everything I could. When I did the "Blondie and Dagwood" movies. I'd always pester the soundman. I learned a lot. I guess that's why I went into telecommunications.

Hawkins: What do you think of all the hubbub about *Life*?

Simms: I'm kind of baffled. I really don't know too much about it. I've never seen the whole movie. But one thing has touched me: when someone told me that *It's a Wonderful Life* really changed his life. He was going to commit suicide, and watching the movie made him realize how important we all are.

Hawkins: I think you had the funniest line I've heard about us kids in *Life*.

Simms: Oh, you mean when they asked about how much we were paid for doing the movie?

Hawkins: Yeah, I was four, Karolyn was six, Carol was ten, and you were twelve. We all had the same agent, and I received $50 a day, Karolyn and Carol got $75, and you received $100.

Simms: I said they must have paid us by the pound. What I think is strange is that everyone still refers to us as "The Kids"—we're the grayest-looking kids I've ever seen. This whole thing is astounding. But what was really strange was when we were at the Motion Picture and Television Home and Hospital in Calabasses, California, about twenty miles from downtown L.A. We were entertaining people and answering questions. Later, I went out back for some fresh air, and I saw a little shop with radio equipment and electronic stuff. I went inside and started talking to this old guy, and he turned out to be the soundman from Columbia when I was working on the "Blondie" films. It just blew me away! Here I was talking with the man who was responsible for me doing what I do today.

Supporting Cast and Crew

TODD KARNS—HARRY BAILEY

Jimmy Hawkins: How did you become an actor?

Todd Karns: My dad was the great character actor Roscoe Karns. I guess it was in my veins.

Hawkins: What was your first experience in pictures?

Karns: It was out at MGM. I did a couple of Andy Hardy movies. In fact, that's when I first worked with Donna Reed. We were both in *The Courtship of Andy Hardy*.

Hawkins: What do you remember about Donna Reed?

Karns: Back at MGM in 1941 and 1942, Donna Reed was very pretty and very mature. I was young and looked maybe fifteen. I had a crush on her, but in the romance department she didn't look my way. She was always a professional and giving actress. I remember her fondly.

Hawkins: Did you know Jimmy Stewart at the time?

Karns: No, but I'd like to share a story with you about Jimmy Stewart that happened off screen. After the MGM movies, I enlisted in the service. In 1943 and 1944, I was stationed at Hobbs, New Mexico, as a medical administrator. At the same time, Jimmy Stewart was taking his advanced training program in heavy bombers. I never met the man but I knew his reputation. When I signed for the role of his brother Harry Bailey, I had the opportunity to meet Mr. Stewart in person. I must say he was the most gracious man and one of the most talented actors I ever met. I learned a lot from him.

Hawkins: How did you get the part of Harry?

Karns: Well, like a lot of actors after the war I was trying to get my career back in gear. I read for Frank Capra, and I guess he saw something in me. The next thing I knew he put me under exclusive contract to his production company. I was supposed to do four pictures a year, but after *Life* Capra's company went belly-up. I was with Liberty for just one year.

Hawkins: What was it like on the first day of shooting *It's a Wonderful Life*?

Karns: Kind of hectic. We were doing the high school gym scene on location at Beverly Hills High. The floor really opens up to a swimming pool! It was a big scene, a lot of activity.

Hawkins: I read a production call sheet on which Alan Hale Jr. was listed as an actor. I never saw him in the movie. Was his scene cut out?

Karns: Oh, no. Alan was signed for the "Hee-Haw" Sam Wainwright part. Well, when Capra started shooting, Alan froze up and had to be replaced. That's when Frank Albertson came in.

Hawkins: What happened to your career after *Life*?

Karns: I left Liberty, and then Leo McCarey signed me to an exclusive contract. I did *Good Sam* for him. TV was coming in, and I did a series with my dad called *Rocky King, Inside Detective* for the old Dumont network. After that I did some other features, including *The Caine Mutiny* with Humphrey Bogart. Then I got interested in painting. My wife and I moved to Mexico, where I've become an artist, but I still act and direct theater down here. Once it's in your blood, you know.

VIRGINIA PATTON—RUTH DAKIN BAILEY

Jimmy Hawkins: I heard you were the only actress under exclusive contract to Frank Capra's Liberty Films.

Virginia Patton: That's right. I wanted to be an actress and joined a small theater group in the Los Angeles area. It was in one of the productions that I was brought to Mr. Capra's attention. My father, my agent, and I were called to his office in Hollywood for an interview, and soon after I was offered a contract.

Hawkins: What do you remember most about filming *It's a Wonderful Life*?

Patton: Being picked to play Jimmy Stewart's sister-in-law. What a vote of confidence, my first role under contract.

Hawkins: Do you have any other memories?

Patton: Frank Capra was always improvising. The scene at the train depot—I think we shot it out in Pasadena. Well, Edward Stevenson, the costume designer, had created an ensemble that included a suit, hat, and white gloves. I had to look good to greet my new brother-in-law. There was a popcorn vendor in the scene, so Capra thought it would be a good idea if I was eating a bag of popcorn. That became a problem for me as an actress—what to do about greasy butter on white gloves. I didn't want to make waves, so I just hoped the camera didn't get close enough to see my gloved hand.

Hawkins: What else do you recall?

Patton: I still haven't gotten over Jimmy Stewart kissing me. In fact, one Christmas my husband and our three children were watching *It's a Wonderful Life*. The children probably missed most of the story line, but they recognized me during the train scene. Their little faces filled with rapt attention until Jimmy Stewart actually hugged and kissed me. My four-year-old said, with utter dismay, "But Mommy, he kissed you. Only Daddy kisses you." My husband took over at that point and tried to explain to our children that this was make-believe. Jimmy Stewart was making believe that he was truly related to me and therefore kissed me as a member of his family. We still chuckle over that one.

BOBBIE ANDERSON—LITTLE GEORGE BAILEY

Jimmy Hawkins: How did you get the role of George Bailey?

Bobbie Anderson: I was under contract with either 20th Century Fox or MGM at the time. Capra chose me and two other boys to read and test for the part. I was recently reminded that Jason Robards Sr.—a close friend of Capra's—fed us our lines. He read the part of Mr. Gower, the part that H. B. Warner played.

I recall that, after I read, he decided to test only me and dismissed the other two. The text was composed of parts of two scenes, one on the ice with the megaphone, teasing my little brother, and the other where I struck the lighter in the drugstore and wished for a million dollars.

After choosing me for the part, I remember he brought Jimmy Stewart in to watch part of the testing and asked what he thought about my performance.

Hawkins: Any memorable moments working with or interacting with the cast?

Anderson: Well, I remember a couple of people who were pretty difficult. Thomas Mitchell was very critical of me if I missed a cue or a line. The harassment got pretty tough, until finally Lionel Barrymore stepped in and told him to relax.

H. B. Warner actually got drunk for the scene in the drugstore and actually hit my ear. We had to rehearse several times,

and after each rehearsal he'd hold me and console me. Capra kept asking me if I was okay, then he'd say, "Let's do it again!"

Hawkins: What was Jimmy Stewart like to you?

Anderson: Well, of course you know I didn't have any scenes with him, but several years later we were working on another picture together, *The Last Hurrah*. I was the second assistant director for the movie and, of course, Jimmy Stewart had a starring role. One day he was in the old coffee shop on the Columbia lot, and when I walked in he looked at me and said, "There's the young George Bailey who helped make one of the best pictures I've ever made." I kind of liked that.

Hawkins: Did you go to the premiere?

Anderson: Yes, I attended with my parents. It was held at the Hollywood Pantages Theatre, and it sticks out quite vividly in my memory. It was quite an elaborate affair as I recall. Some of the ushers and young people in the audience came over afterward and congratulated me. It was the first time I really received public recognition for a part I played. Even after playing bigger parts, this was the most recognized of my career.

Hawkins: What else do you remember?

Anderson: Well, there's the Barrymore story. A few years later, when I was in high school, I became good friends with John Barrymore Jr., the grandson of Lionel Barrymore. Because of a family split with John Sr. and the divorce from Ethel, the family became estranged from the old patriarch, Lionel. We had some crazy and dangerous times together as kids.

Years later I ran into John when I was working as an assistant director at Desilu. He was acting in a production there, and Argyle Nelson, the head of production, asked me to come down to the set on the Gene Autry ranch. Since Argyle knew John and I were friends, he thought I might be the one to talk him out of burning down a set barn. He just wanted to burn it down and wouldn't go back to work until they let him do it. I don't remember what I said to John, but he didn't burn the barn down and went back to work. God, those were wild times we used to have.

Hawkins: After sixty years in the movie business, how would you sum it up? Has it been a wonderful life?

Anderson: Yes and no. It's always been a love/hate relationship between myself and the film industry. It's been good to me overall, but the business has changed remarkably in the last fifteen years or so. The family environment and sense of loyalty is gone now and the politicking involved has become extremely aggressive—sometimes it's even ugly. However, if I consider filmmaking in its purest sense, my love for that creative, exhilarating forum hasn't waned one iota.

SHELDON LEONARD—NICK THE BARTENDER

Sheldon Leonard went on to become a successful writer, producer, and director of such programs as the *Danny Thomas, Andy Griffith,* and *Dick Van Dyke* shows.

Jimmy Hawkins: You've directed a lot of successful shows. How did you find Frank Capra as a director?

Sheldon Leonard: Well, I acted in two of Capra's movies, *It's a Wonderful Life* and *Pocketful of Miracles.* We also worked together at the Directors Guild. In both situations he was sharp when dealing with difficult problems.

Hawkins: How was he on the set of *It's a Wonderful Life*?

Leonard: He was very tolerant, observant, and even-tempered. He would go over everything in a scene until it was just right. Then and only then would we put it on film.

Hawkins: What did you think of the kind of films Capra made?

Leonard: Both of the movies I did have become holiday classics. People like them more now than when they were originally released. There is a need for sentimental movies.

Hawkins: Was there any talk during production that a classic was in the making?

Leonard: There was no hint of future greatness. We felt we were just doing another movie. Whatever hurt the film when it was initially released is responsible for its success today.

ARGENTINA BRUNETTI—MRS. MARTINI

Jimmy Hawkins: How did you get the part of Mrs. Martini?

Argentina Brunetti: My agent, Lew Sherrell, sent me out to Culver City to meet with Frank Capra. We spoke about my stage background. Mr. Capra knew my mother, Mimi Aguglina, who was a famous Italian actress, and he just looked at me and said, "Okay, you're it. If you're Mimi's daughter, you must be okay." And that was it.

Hawkins: What do you remember most about being on the set?

Brunetti: *It's a Wonderful Life* was only my third or fourth motion picture, so I was very excited.

Hawkins: How was Frank Capra to work with?

Brunetti: When Mr. Capra yelled "Action!" everything happened. The lights went on and he lived the excitement of the scene. He knew every line and repeated them to himself. He lived those characters.

In the last scene of the movie, when Jimmy Stewart was happy with the whole town bringing him money and he knew he was going to be saved, Mr. Capra was watching the whole scene as if he were living it himself, as if it were happening to him. Tears were flowing down his cheeks. I couldn't believe it! I was more enthralled watching him than the scene.

Hawkins: Do you remember any incidents during filming?

Brunetti: Oh, I remember the snow on the set. They said it was made especially for the movie. Well, I slipped on it, but not while I was filming. It was wonderful. I enjoyed it very much!

Hawkins: Did you keep in touch with Mr. Capra?

Brunetti: Yes, I visited him in La Quinta right before his wife died. He told me the reason he stopped directing was because he got those terrible headaches and he wanted to be with his wife. He was a kind man.

ELLEN CORBY—MRS. DAVIS

Jimmy Hawkins: How did you get involved in doing *It's a Wonderful Life*?

Ellen Corby: It was my very first movie as an actress. For about twelve years before *It's a Wonderful Life* I had been a script supervisor. I had worked behind the camera with some fine directors, but Frank Capra was head and shoulders above them all. He was the best.

Hawkins: How did he direct you in the "run on the bank" scene, when everyone wants their money back?

Corby: He didn't say much, but he was an inspiration. I had only one line. I don't even think it was scripted. Mr. Capra told me to say "I think seventeen dollars." We rehearsed it and then filmed it a couple of times. Then before the next take Mr. Capra

"It's a Wonderful Life"

By Mary Jo Slater

I first became aware of "It's a Wonderful Life" when I saw it on late night television as a twelve year old. I used to stay up all night watching old movies. The message the movie left me with has been the guiding force of my life. Every person has value and a reason for existing. I believe that the film gave me a sense of purpose.

At age nineteen, I moved to New York City to study acting. I always dreamed of being a part of the entertainment business. I believe "It's a Wonderful Life" opened the door to my dreams. The film gave me a sense of self-worth. Moving took courage, but I knew my destiny lay elsewhere. I met and married an actor. One of us had to pay the bills so I became an agent. This led me to a job with a famous Broadway producer where I started producing off-Broadway plays. I started to wonder about the possibility of turning "It's a Wonderful Life" into a Broadway musical. It seemed like a natural progression and I wondered why no one had ever attempted to make a musical of the film. I tracked down Philip Van Doren Stern. He was so impressed by my passion for the idea of turning the movie into a musical that he gave me a copy of this original short story entitled "The Greatest Gift."

I approached several famous lyricists and composers to write the score, but something always happened and they would decide not to become involved. Finally, my dear friend and Broadway producer, Eugene Wolsk, decided to help me. He brought his old friend Sheldon Harnick on board. After several months of negotiations with Sheldon's attorneys, he was finally committed. Next we had to find a composer, Joe Raposo who had success writing songs for Frank Sinatra, Barbra Streisand, and "Sesame Street" seemed a great choice. He was excited about the idea. We did a great workshop production that Tom O'Horgan of "Hair" fame directed. We felt confident that the money would come easily and that the show was just what Broadway needed. Well, we were wrong. Everyone liked the show, but no one wanted to take a risk on a sweet old-fashioned musical. We were up against the era of Andrew Lloyd Weber and his successful show "Cats," so warm-hearted shows were not what was selling.

We performed our musical at the University of Michigan where it received raves from the local critics. Still a long way from the Great White Way. Sadly, Joe Raposo passed away not long after this production but he did fulfill his dream of seeing a full-scale production performed. A dream come true for most of us.

Shortly after moving my family to Los Angeles, I met an actor named Doug Rowe who ran a community theater in Laguna, California. He was excited by the idea of working on an original musical with a respected lyricist like Sheldon. We auditioned actors and found a perfect George Bailey in Ralph Bruneau. From this production, another actor friend, Casey Biggs, came to see it and told a friend who ran the Arena Stage in Washington about the production. We received mixed reviews from the critics, but the audiences came and cried and cheered after each performance. I realized that this was a musical for average people (like the Baileys)—not for hard-core critics. Our hope is that someday it will go to Broadway. I will never give up. I believe if you want something badly enough, you can make dreams come true. Mine have so far and I hope they will continue to come true in the future. I am so grateful for my exposure to "It's a Wonderful Life." I wish the film would be required viewing in all elementary schools across the land. I believe it could impact many young lives as it did mine.

came up to me and whispered a different amount for me to say. I did, and that surprised Jimmy Stewart and changed the rhythm of the scene. Jimmy looked at me, grabbed my face, and kissed me. Then I was surprised. The whole scene played better, and so did our performances, just because Mr. Capra was so creative.

ALBERT HACKETT—SCREENWRITER

Jimmy Hawkins: How did you get involved in writing *It's a Wonderful Life*?

Albert Hackett: Well, my wife and writing partner, Frances Goodrich, and I had just finished writing *The Virginian* when Capra hired us to do *It's a Wonderful Life*.

We didn't have much to do with Capra. He said what he wanted and then we'd go off and do it. We would work things out—"try this, do that." My wife always felt Capra couldn't wait to write it himself. She really didn't like him.

Hawkins: Why not?

Hackett: He kind of disappointed us. We heard he was working with other writers while we were still on the project. The whole process is like a rag. You keep wringing the story out until nothing is left—except what you see on the screen. He told us to hurry up and finish it. We wrote the last scene and never saw Frank after that.

Hawkins: Were there any bad feelings?

Hackett: We never did another project together. The Writers Guild arbitrated the script and Frank ended up with screenplay credit. The only thing that matters is what's up there on the screen. In all fairness, it's Capra's film all the way.

EMILE KURI—SET DECORATOR

Jimmy Hawkins: I like to start by asking everyone how he or she got involved with the film.

Emile Kuri: I was under exclusive contract to Liberty Films. It's kind of funny how I came to Capra. I had done a lot of work for Selznick, and we were also personal friends. There was a strike, and the union sent me to Selznick Studios to walk the picket line. I told them I couldn't do that to Selznick: "Send me to walk some other studio!" I was fined about $2,500—a lot of money back in the mid-1940s. I paid it, but they wouldn't reinstate me. That's when Capra and Liberty Films stepped in. They wanted me under exclusive contract, but I was in hot water with the union. Liberty tried talking to the union, but no dice. Then we went to court and sued. I won the case and also an exclusive contract with Liberty.

Hawkins: Then did you start work on *It's a Wonderful Life*?

Kuri: No, the script wasn't finished yet. So Liberty loaned me out to do a Hitchcock film, I think. When that was over *It's a Wonderful Life* was ready.

Hawkins: What was the first thing you did as a set decorator?

Kuri: We had to figure out the size of Bedford Falls. Everyone agreed it would be a population of 30,000 people. Main Street would be three blocks long.

Hawkins: Was that built at the RKO ranch in Encino?

Kuri: Yes, it was built exclusively for *It's a Wonderful Life*.

Hawkins: What was your biggest problem?

Kuri: We had to age the town. The movie starts when the Jimmy Stewart character is a young boy in the 1920s. Then a few years pass and he's going to go to college. The years in between meant the store windows had to reflect those changes. Trees taller, new vehicles, houses, and neon signs. Then we see the Main Street in the summer of 1943 during World War II. Then it goes to that winter. Rain and snow had to be brought in. We even brought in dogs, cats, pigeons, and other animals months before principal photography began so they would feel at home. Capra didn't miss a thing.

Hawkins: What did you do to change the town when George's wish is granted?

Kuri: The whole town had to be different. We had to show how it would have been without George Bailey's influence.

Remember, he helped families through hard times with his Building & Loan Company. The town wasn't Bedford Falls anymore, it was Pottersville, and it had to reflect Potter's corruption. Now it was full of saloons and brothels. It was a company town with everyone out for himself. The seeds of kindness from George Bailey were missing.

Hawkins: How was Capra to work with?

Kuri: He didn't say much. I'd show him how I thought things should look. He spoke to me and made me feel that he was appreciative of all the work I had done.

JOSEPH BIROC—CAMERAMAN

Jimmy Hawkins: How did you first get involved in *It's a Wonderful Life*?

Joseph Biroc: I was the camera operator right from the beginning. I did all the makeup and wardrobe tests with Vic Milner, the first cinematographer.

Hawkins: Then did you become the cinematographer?

Biroc: Capra and Vic Milner didn't get along very well. Frank had always worked with Joe Walker, but Joe was over at Columbia and couldn't get away. Capra thought Milner worked too slowly, and the crew thought he was too authoritative.

Hawkins: Is that why Milner left the picture?

Biroc: Well, he could get away with that attitude with the crew. But he made the mistake of doing it to Capra. Milner told Capra to leave the set until he was ready. Capra said it was his set and if Milner didn't like it he could leave. So Vic left!

Next thing I knew, Joe Walker was there. He reshot the big street scenes. I later found out that Joe told Capra to start training me to take over because he would be leaving in five or six weeks to start a Rosalind Russell film at Columbia.

Hawkins: How did you find out that you would be the cinematographer?

Biroc: Capra came to me when I was sitting on the camera crane and said, "How would you like to take over the picture?" I said, "Wonderful!" He said, "Okay, it's yours."

Hawkins: What was the set like after you took over?

Biroc: Real jovial! Never a dull moment. Capra was really sharp and knew what he wanted. He'd listen to my ideas and was very generous. I received screen credit along with Joe Walker as a photographer.

When the movie came out, it was regarded as mediocre. Now, after all the films I've ever done, *It's a Wonderful Life* is the longest-lived one. My first movie as a full-fledged cameraman. It's an American classic

BOB LAWLESS—SPECIAL EFFECTS CREW MEMBER

Jimmy Hawkins: How did you get involved with *It's a Wonderful Life*?

Bob Lawless: I was on the labor gang at RKO, a group of guys who went from one picture to another. I got a call to report to the RKO ranch in Encino. It was about a half-hour ride from the main lot in Hollywood.

Hawkins: What did they have you doing?

Lawless: My job was to make snow for the movie. I loaded ice into the machine that sprayed the snow all over the street Jimmy Stewart was running down.

Hawkins: How did they make the snow?

Lawless: Special-effects man Russell Shearman worked with his RKO staff and created an innovative new snow-making technique. The purest driven snow came out of nozzles under very high pressure. When it blew through the wind machines at different speeds, it could be soft and fluffy or raging like a blizzard. When used as a ground covering, the new snow looked slushy, as though it had been walked through, driven over, and then lain around town for a while. It was no problem to work with because it didn't have any odor and was harmless to clothes, paint, wood, and people, which followed Hollywood's usual order of economic priority.

The day they began shooting the snowstorm it was eighty-four degrees, and by noon it was in the nineties. The snow, however, remained hard and cold-looking. Everyone stood around to watch despite the heat. Altogether, the winter scenes used 300 tons of plaster—250 tons of it to build up snow banks and fifty to spray in the snow mixture. Window sills were covered with gypsum. Snow paths and rutted car tracks were made out of 3,000 tons of shaved ice. *It's a Wonderful Life* would use more snow than any picture since *Lost Horizon*. The special effects crew spent three weeks getting ready to create the snowstorm. Their job was to cover all four acres of Bedford Falls with snow. Besides the shaved ice and gypsum, they used 6,000 gallons of chemicals for the new film snow, which replaced crunchy white cornflakes.

Hawkins: Did the snow win any awards?

Lawless: Yes, the Motion Picture Academy gave Russell Shearman and the RKO Special Effects Department a Class III citation for "development of a new method of simulating fallen snow."

DIMITRI TIOMKIN—MUSICAL SCORE

Jimmy Hawkins: How did Mr. Tiomkin become involved with *It's a Wonderful Life*?

John Waxman [President of Themes and Variations, and con-

servator for the Dimitri Tiomkin estate]: Mr. Capra and Mr. Tiomkin worked together on *Lost Horizon*, in 1937.

Hawkins: So if *It's a Wonderful Life* wasn't their first collaboration, what was?

Waxman: They worked together on six movies, and during World War II they did the "Why We Fight Series." But *It's a Wonderful Life* was their last project together.

Hawkins: Why?

Waxman: Mr. Tiomkin's score was very complex, with rich orchestrations. Before the movie was released Mr. Capra deleted many of Tiomkin's cues and replaced them with works by Alfred Newman, Leigh Harline, and Roy Webb from the RKO music library. These replacements hurt Mr. Tiomkin very much.

Hawkins: What cues were deleted?

Waxman: Mr. Tiomkin suggested "Ode to Joy" for the final scene, but that was replaced with "Auld Lang Syne."

Hawkins: How did Mr. Tiomkin feel that affected the theme?

Waxman: The theme that Mr. Tiomkin was looking for was a theme of unity—"All together, we are one." "Auld Lang Syne" translates to "friends remember friends." Capra's disregard for Tiomkin's choice shattered their friendship. They never worked together again.

Hawkins: How has the music from *Life* lived on?

Waxman: Through a concert suite. Since it was first intro-duced to audiences throughout the country it has become a staple of Christmas concerts in diverse parts of the country. I can think of no higher tribute to the universal appeal of the film than the annual performances of the music by community, regional, and major orchestras throughout our country.

Hawkins: What was the most touching request you received regarding Tiomkin's score?

Waxman: In 1992 Steve Ross, president of Warner Com-munications, died. His wife requested that the music from his favorite film, *It's a Wonderful Life,* be played at the memorial service in his honor.

Hawkins: I heard that since Steve Ross was such a fan, when he checked into the hospital for the last time, he didn't want anyone to know he was there so he registered under an assumed name: George Bailey.

Behind the set of "It's a Wonderful Life," with cameraman Joe Biroc and Ward Bond (at right, with sunglasses).

Life after Life

On May 16, 1947, Frank Capra sold Liberty Films to Paramount Pictures for close to one million dollars. Frank Capra signed a deal to make three films for Paramount, with a salary cap of $156,000 per picture and no profit participation. In signing this contract Frank Capra gave up any stake in *It's a Wonderful Life* forever.

In the 1950s, *It's a Wonderful Life* was re-released to theaters. Then a distribution company, M. & A. Alexander, acquired the copyright and film to add to its enormous library. Alexander sold its films to National Television Association (NTA).

Television made this movie a classic. Whenever someone turned on the television, day and night, *It's a Wonderful Life* was on.

At first the film had a cult following. People held theme parties, *It's a Wonderful Life* trivia became the rage, and, most important, families would get together to share the movie's message. The late 1980s were a time when viewers were bombarded with the movie. It aired on almost every independent station in every market. In 1990 stations in Los Angeles showed the movie eleven times during Christmas Eve and Christmas Day.

Although television made *It's a Wonderful Life* a success, Capra's frustration was immense. He was not benefiting from the popularity of his film. A glimmer of hope (or Capra's own guardian angel) appeared in the form of Hal Roach Studios, which wanted to colorize the film. Capra knew that if the film were colorized it could be copyrighted again and he could gain from it. He entered into an agreement to put up half the cost in exchange for half the profits. Capra later changed his mind and became a spokesperson for the Directors Guild against the colorization of films.

Although the movie sells more than 600,000 video copies a year, NBC's televised showing was so well received in 1994 that NBC exercised its option to televise it during the 1995 and 1996 holiday seasons.

A Letter from Frank Capra Jr.

My dad's film, "It's a Wonderful Life," has constantly given our family such inspiration and support. Just as it has for so many others in the world. We not only watch it at Christmas time but at least once or twice more during the year. Everyone has their down and dark moments, just as George Bailey did, and there is nothing more inspiring and uplifting than to be caught up in the experience of this wonderful film. Beyond these feelings, there is also the great pride and love for my dad which I always feel when watching the movie. It is so much a part of him and he is so much a part of it. The story, the writing, the film making, everything about it is at his highest level and it always remained his favorite film. "The one film I was born to make" is what he said to me once. Over the years he received so many personal responses and accolades from all over the world as the movie was seen more and more. He was delighted for it to be so strongly received on television and home video and to see it grow in popularity with his audience "the people" each year. We miss him every day, but seeing his films and especially "It's a Wonderful Life" brings him back to us each time.

Cast and Crew Credits

An RKO Picture. A Liberty Film Production produced and directed by Frank Capra. Screenplay by Frances Goodrich, Albert Hackett, and Frank Capra. Additional scenes by Jo Swerling. Based on a story by Philip Van Doren Stern. Musical score written and directed by Dimitri Tiomkin. Directors of Photography: Joseph Walker and Joseph Biroc. Special photographic effects by Russell A. Cully. Art director: Jack Okey. Set decoration: Emile Kuri. Makeup supervision: Gordon Bau. Film Editor: William Hornbeck. Sound by Richard Van Hessen and Clem Portman. Costumes by Edward Stevenson. Assistant Director: Arthur S. Black.

CAST

George Bailey: James Stewart

Mary Hatch: Donna Reed

Mr. Potter: Lionel Barrymore

Uncle Billy: Thomas Mitchell

Clarence: Henry Travers

Mrs. Bailey: Beulah Bondi

Ernie: Frank Faylen

Bert: Ward Bond

Violet: Gloria Grahame

Mr. Gower: H. B. Warner

Harry Bailey: Todd Karns

Peter Bailey: Samuel S. Hinds

Cousin Millie: Mary Treen

Sam Wainwright: Frank Albertson

Ruth Dakin: Virginia Patton

Cousin Eustace: Charles Williams

Mrs. Hatch: Sarah Edwards

Mr. Martini: William Edmunds

Mrs. Martini: Argentina Brunetti

Annie: Lillian Randolph

Little George: Bobbie Anderson

Little Sam: Ronnie Ralph

Little Mary: Jean Gale

Little Violet: Jeanine Anne Roose

Little Marty Hatch: Danny Mummert

Little Harry Bailey: Georgie Nokes

Nick: Sheldon Leonard

Potter's Bodyguard: Frank Hagney

Joe (Luggage shop): Ray Walker

Real Estate Salesman: Charles Lane

Tom (Building & Loan): Edward Keen

The Bailey Children

Janie Bailey: Carol Coombs

Zuzu Bailey: Karolyn Grimes

Pete Bailey: Larry Simms

Tommy Bailey: Jimmy Hawkins

Carter, Bank Examiner: Charles Halton

Tollhouse Keeper: Tom Fadden

High School Principal: Harry Holman

Mr. Welch: Stanley Andrews

Marty Hatch: Hal Landon

Freddie: Carl "Alfalfa" Switzer

Mickey: Bobby Scott

Doctor Campbell: Harry Cheshire

Bank Teller: Ed Featherstone

Owner of House: J. Farrell MacDonald

Bill Poster: Gary Owen

Mrs. Wainwright: Marian Carr

Mrs. Davis: Ellen Corby

Mr. Potter's Secretary: Almira Sessions

Angel's Voices

Joseph: Joseph Granby

Franklin: Maroni Olsen

Violet (Gloria Grahame) thanks George for the money to leave town and go to the big city.

George begs Uncle Billy to remember where he lost the money.

Above: The family shows concern for their dad's stern demeanor and little Tommy tugs for his attention.

Right: The Bailey family puts holiday cheer on hold as George's desperation causes worry.

Above: Peter asks his father for spelling advice.
Right: George, Zuzu, and her petals.

Opposite: Mary and the children question George's mood.

Left: Mr. Martini (William Edmunds) begs George to go home moments before he is punched by Mr. Welch (Stanley Andrews).

Below: Nick (Sheldon Leonard) and Mr. Martini help George to his feet.

Opposite: George is suspicious of Clarence (Henry Travers), the newest addition to his life.

Left: George finally realizes that Clarence is more than just a friendly visitor.

Below: George decides to go to Bailey Park in search of his friends.

Bert (Ward Bond) listens to ecstatic George rave about Zuzu's petals.

ASPETUCK
KITCHAWAN
←
KATONAH
CHAPPAQUA
→

George runs down the streets of Bedford Falls

George's family celebrates his return.

The town of Bedford Falls comes

All is well again at the Bailey household.